to the heart i
carry, full of
loss and ache.

A Poet's Degree in Suffering

Poetry & Prose

By: karnes

the older i get, the more torn i am between wanting to be with someone and wanting to be free. i don't know if there is such a thing or such a world where they coexist. i understand love can be freedom in and of itself, and any form of it will hand you a particular part of yourself you didn't know existed. there's simply too much desire in my body for travel, writing, and solitude. i struggle with a dedicated concept of pairing what i want with what someone else wants. during the last several years of not being able to explore as much and being a hostage with everything going on in this country and around the world, i've felt pieces of me slip away. we won't ever get back the time we waste. we won't ever get back overthinking where we should be, when we know exactly where that's at. each one of us has it inside of us, a destination only known to ourselves. i'm grateful to be here, still pondering life's mysteries and questions. the unsettled ache in my life is a yearning to be somewhere else, not with anyone else. as much as i revere love and write about having someone to hold, i think at my core, i'm a human in search of experience through encounters and conversations with as many strangers that walk with this earth. i want to know everyone i can and hear their stories. i want to experience everyone and meet them at their best and worst. an inconceivable act of living, i know. nobody will ever come close to doing it. i have time left to try. being a writer, i think that's what's most important. being able to not necessarily connect with another, but meeting them at a familiar place and creating a moment out of it to share and sit with when everything else around me feels as if it is leaving. it is the defined act of living in my opinion. the way one talks to you, absolutely tells you all you need to know about them and yourself. it is a reflection of safety they see and find in you, being around you, and being able to stomach an hour long discussion about nothing, about everything. we are too scared to speak openly about what we want, even though we know it will be with us when we go to sleep and wake up. we never get around to releasing our feelings, because we may not want to burden someone else with it or we are just too fucking dim to value our own light. wherever you are in this life, know you are good enough for anything, even a conversation between another when you feel silence may be the best language to use.

at this point in my life, i am after peace more than love, more than someone to come back to after my travels. if i am honest with myself, i am better off alone tending to the road in front of me, watching a sun rise and slowly vanish to walk its own path again. i do not belong here. i am sure of it. it's the only thing i am sure of these days. my writing is my mirror, my confessional, my truest center. it is the place where judgment is absent, away from those who believe living is staying in one place and calling it home. i belong to the elements, to the vacancy residing in me, begging for a benevolent fulfillment. give me a piece of paper from the ground to the sky and i'll write you a poem that never ends. it will be a first of its kind. it will be the first time a poet didn't abandon his work to begin to love something else in order to find his heart and lose his mind.

darling, you were meant to be brave.

now show them. reckless is a word only

used by those who lost their soul for

something they truly loved.

we will get there if we continue pushing

through the bad days. the days when getting

out of bed hurts. the days when your soul

is too tired for your body to hold.

may the art always survive. may it become a never-ending guide for others to use when they feel all is lost, even when the humanity they are surrounded by goes into hiding. without pain, loss, agony, a tender brokenness, there would be nothing everlasting to show for it, if not for the brave who share their devastation in hopes of rekindling the ashes they're left with.

i may be nothing more than a misplaced

human in search of a place others tell me

doesn't exist, but i know where i'm going.

take these roots and place them as deep as you can in the blue of you. my hands no longer work the way they once did. holding thorns and wrestling with horns makes living a sacred dance between the marriage of flesh and bone. i'm not a lover these days. i'll break anything just to feel something, just to feel what not missing you is like.

i know it isn't easy waking up and hoping things get easier. i have been cursed to witness an array of truths greet me, only to fall beside me, afraid of their own shadow. howl and cry out if you need to. sometimes, we must release the animal to feel a bit more human in a cruel world.

take time for yourself. when i say that, what i mean is to take care of your minutes, hours, weeks, months, and years. without accepting the day, we will never be able to dream openly and love without fear of losing what will one day become an extension of who we used to be, of who we have grown to be.

A Poet's Degree in Suffering

hiding out in-between a pause and thought, i relish days when nothing happens, where shine outweighs pain. i've lived a long life of regret forming on the inside of my hands, when i could've held you longer, but i ended up losing you instead. poetry is a delicate balance of unraveling while maintaining some sort of humanly form. i don't do it to be heard or seen. i do it to justify a gift someone once gave to me. my eyes melt into a sunny parade of balloons and hallucinogens comprised of every room i've locked myself in to survive a night that surely was meant to destroy anyone in my life. you entangled yourself amongst my words, and now, i do my best to write you softly, finely, simply.

maybe there is life beyond our clench,
a way towards finding us and everything
all over again. you've become the words
and body to my breath. as long as
the moon remains above and brightly,
there will always be a moment when
i feel you close to me.

there's still a pain in my voice i'm trying to name. lodged between a stone and poem tucked neatly into the corner of my throat. love can be ruthless, a coroner's wet dream. most days, missing you is all it takes for me to orchestrate birds to sing its melody. morning crawls to me and night is its teacher. a blue sky is my reminder how storms are colorless when trying to find peace within eyes that remain full of all the memories it leaves behind.

i do not know how to speak appropriately, so i use my typewriter as my jaw, my speech, my tongue. it is the extension of everything i am and used to be. the good and bad live at my fingertips, shaking and tapping their way out of a mind that has locked away my ability to remember how it feels to accept the love i deserve.

we don't always get what we want or hope
for. more times than not, we get nothing
but an unannounced beauty to spend the rest
of our lives trying to define, trying to
place amongst everything else that's left.

war gave me my rage, but your
love comforted all of my self-hatred
and the devil in me. some humans
do not want to change you. they want
to hold you just as you are.

to know pain is to have known love. it is a relentless cycle, a repetitive act of losing yourself and forgetting what was taught, shown, and given, prior to this day.

we could've been a lot of things, but all we will ever be are songs we once found each other in. the same songs others will learn to love and sing together, harmoniously in sync with hearts wide open, unknowingly inching closer to an end they will never see coming until it is over.

not all things are meant to last.
some things only occur to show you
what can happen when you least
expect change.

find me when you cannot find yourself.

i'll be there for you, as a breath,

as an interval, as a settled body

to hold when you feel nothing

but letting go.

i've always wanted more than others.
maybe not so much love as to
just more wandering. my life needs
fluidity, a certain mobility to flex
out of my skin for a while. being human
all day is exhausting, so i do my
best taking my time when it comes to
my personal relationship with everything
around me.

i never knew how to be anything more than who i was before you. a lifetime of wondering has left me scattered amongst a less assorted form of an assembled ensemble of perfection. i am nothing, if i'm not to be yours, boundlessly.

sit and talk with the moon as often as you can. you will learn more about life and love than with anything else you give your time to. we are only here for a short while. i hope you believe in the magic of conversation and finally being heard.

may this soul shine on in an infinite
way, in a starry surrender of casual
rage. take the darkness if you must,
but leave me the victory.

may love know you fully. may it be aware of all your dreams and desires. make room for anything permanent, anything that says your name gently and you believe in it, finally.

i've been on this path, this way of life
since my mother looked at me and called me,
son. i've been on this path, this journey
since my father looked at me and called me,
son. i've been on this path, this journey
since i first saw what war could do to you
once you made it back home.

i hope you know your place in this universe. i hope you never put yourself second to anything. firstly and lastly, it comes to you. the belief you have and how to show others what makes you who you are, is where the magic happens, where the growth becomes a rising tide of understanding self over valuing what others think of you.

you may never know anything but solitude,
and if you're lucky, you'll find the love
you need inside of its edges. we all are
destined for something. some of us are
called upon to redefine what love is.

release anything that isn't serving you in a wholesome manner. we are the only proof of coming back from a certain death love gave us when we thought it was against us in the beginning.

love may never feel like this again, as if the sun itself fell from the sky and landed in your heart and eyes. there is a fire the gods once spoke about. i am trying to remember how not to run away, but remain firmly pressed against an unending sensation of unexpected and righteous alignment.

take me to the places you'll always see and

find yourself. tell me about them all so

i will be able to never go a day without

you when distance cuts in line

and separates us.

there was a time when nothing hurt and all things were a type of beauty that felt like waking from a winter's slumber. i hope you find more days like these and less of the snow covering your eyes and mouth.

A Poet's Degree in Suffering

i'm after more than the stars show to me in my darkness. i am only lost when i am way from you, away from the soul we share. if there were to be a me without you, take my name and face away. i do not belong to this place if it is not by your side.

do not go gently without fighting for what you love. too often we bend at the knee to appease a crowd that would rather see us beheaded than living with a mind of our own.

grant yourself the love and permission to go beyond your limits. it is only then do we grow beyond the horizon we see. only then do we outgrow the oaks and pines taking our light away. take in all you can while you can. many believe tomorrow is a reality when today is barely a whispered thing.

i know life can be difficult even for the strongest of warriors. take time for yourself when you feel as thought it is collapsing. we can always build again, wholly and fully.

i've felt you before; in the waves,

in the birds above, under every

nightly moon. this life of mine

was always leading me closer

to the woman you've fought to

become and love.

to the mistakes that raised me, to the room that housed me. to the hearts that broke mine, to the moon that shaped me. to the laughs that saved me, to the woman who loved me though my darkened days. to the scars that made me, to the lost and forgotten that never left me. i'm someone who never should have made it this far, but even in my infancy, i remained larger than life.

i'm always going to have the marks of the moon on me. some humans leave you with more than what had to give. i'm never going to be the same, but at least i knew you when i barely knew myself. you'll always be the wish i keep secretly and safe. it's the last thing i can be selfish about when it comes to you.

there is still snow on the ground by the graves. a reminder of a coldness of how all living things find their way back to us. we walked for a few miles, a circular journey of all life and all love. i was amazed by the landscape, the immense imprint of burial sites. if you linger long enough, you will know the story of who you are better.

i hope you are able to know someone who values your presence and misses you enough to tell you how much of their world disappears when you are gone. i hope you know how beautiful it is to be with another who has waited years to feel seen, to feel anything other than the one always trying to make things work. your heart deserves to be kept safe inside of something other than a suitcase.

they couldn't burn you then. they can't burn you now. the mother of moons. the daughter of magic. the fire within a wolf's soul. you may have been tied to the stake, but your wild set you free. a true representation of Hecate, your wrath goes beyond hell-hounds and ghosts. when night comes, you'll feast and reign again.

i'll write until the trees force me to leave their forests and begin giving back to myself instead of stealing away more of their rings to give to you. all of these years, you've been the muse and rose. the love and throne. i've gotten older and taller, but in my mind, you're still how i found you, outlasting time and as beautiful as you were making a sunrise blush before you became mine. even when you're seventy, a youthfulness will exude from you, keeping the ocean blue and stars infinitely alive.

some things aren't made for forever. some things are better off felt long enough to know everything can be real if you try at it, if you want it to be a part of your life. we will never get a say as to how long things will last. sometimes, it is nothing more than a, hello. which if you're lucky enough to get, goodbye is surely to follow. welcome to earth, sweet child, where many welcome lonely because love is an unknown parcel of land inside a heart no one will ever fully understand.

my joy was stolen years ago. happiness tried to take its place, but when two things are forced to cooperate and collaborate, nothing will survive. as a child, it didn't take much for me to smile. i wasn't sure i knew what sadness was until my parents showed me what it looked like, until they told me it wasn't my fault. i put blame on myself often for things i had no control over. years later, i have yet to learn how to live without doing it all the time. i struggle to find anything to wrap my arms around. the dead weight i carry makes it impossible not to care for those around me, for those who hurt inside as i do. i'll continue to love, because love taught me how to hold on, how to reflect, and how to let go of every breath i had saved for you.

and when they leave, i hope they don't take the best parts of you with them. i hope you are able to move forward with your soul still intact and with fluidity of a single stream raging onward. i know it may feel as though death is closing in, asking you if you're ready. i hope your courage allows you to rip out its backbone and use it to help you walk even further. we are not what they do to us. we are the love they didn't know what to do with. there is tragedy in every story. the biggest one oftentimes is believing the fault falls at our knees when they had left a long time before leaving you feeling responsible.

i still have a memory of you to pick from. an endless array of infinite choosing. a hotel meeting, sitting in the restaurant parking lot having lunch in your car, talking about anything to make the day longer than the goodbye that would stay with us. i could say i don't remember anything, but i am living with everything without you. moving on gets easier after the ending or so they tell me. they aren't the ones watching you live your life with what i wanted to give. happiness is an illusion where two people collide without the intrusion. it's an illustrious confusion between a heart teaching a mind it's okay to allow ghosts to haunt your home. i've been running in circles around the circles you left behind. i never wanted it to be like this, but love is the only entity that can stop and rewind time. my joy is knowing you're okay, even if there are days i am not even close to knowing what that feels like or who i am anymore. you can keep the stars. i'll keep the scars. i'll be here, full of what you gave me. you kept me from starving, when all of the wolves went into hiding.

there was never a day when i wasn't trying to love the sorrow out of you. i knew how much of your life left you in a disappointed state. i didn't want to become another box full of memories for you to keep. some of us are destined to be reminders and others are meant to be what remains. i was birthed as a stowaway. i am all too familiar with runaways, which is how i know staying is only for the sun and moon. we never had a chance of making it. we both came from the same place where abandonment is the only form of love given to children of broken hearts.

i know you've been through more hell and every stage of grief known to anyone who risks it all for love, for a greater chance at beginning again. i hope you never feel compelled to worry about what others think of you, because what matters most in the end, is how full you can make your own heart without needing anything else to be proud of. in order to move on, you must bury the dead you keep alive and the angst from being broken by those who told you they loved you, only to drive the knife deeper inside. you are the wolf and the moon.

in her dreams, she goes back to the little girl who met herself for the first time. she wasn't always cautious, but living becomes exhausting when even those you trust keep taking without ever running to you when you ask for help. you know who you are when the night begs of you to stay. you have always had trouble sleeping and calming that locomotive mind of yours. a glass of wine helps, but you are more of the entire bottle type. there is no judgment for being that way. some of us don't dream enough, and it shows. small minds tend to be reserved for those who do the most harm to not only life itself, but those they don't understand. full moons bring the best out in you. loving too much is the only proof we have that shows we are capable of living fully. yours is on display infinitely, as the sun kneels next to the gods who gave their immortality away so you could live on forever.

A Poet's Degree in Suffering

i wish for more blood in my sunrises and less normalcy in these begging eyes. i awake in the shape of a crooked "R" most days and end up alone without conversation to straighten these thrawn and meandering bones i am made of. i want to say by the fifth day i heard you speak about how you got your name. i remember smiling, because i told you how often it rarely occurs to me to show someone my softer side of human. i'm not cold blooded. my fire went out years ago when winter brought a frost i couldn't shake off. it's been a torturing season. the type of longing that will bring bears out of hibernation and make birds sing for Johnny because June went missing. i've done the cocaine and whiskey, the pills and cigarettes. nothing comes close to living as loving you once did.

A Poet's Degree in Suffering

i wake up and roll to the edge of your memory. i think to myself how not to die today, how to keep living with a highway running in-between white lines and caution signs. i make it halfway through my day before i realize you are gone, before my own life betrays me and anxiety becomes a dance partner i am tired of seeing outlast every goddamn song the band plays. there's a fine line between heaven and hell. mine used to be you. it kept me from sinking below my rage, the redness of a devil's flame. i used to believe i wasn't any good without you, but that was another lie i fished out to make you hurting me hurt less because i loved you beyond reason, beyond a vision no one could see but my blinded heart. you were once a comforting force. now there's a suffocated noise gasping from a body, looking for an answer only suffering can embody. meaning something to someone else doesn't matter if you cannot find worth in your own damn life.

the truth is, i'd never be able to see you again. i know i'd hold you and tell you i love you one more time or a thousand times if there were enough minutes in our fleeting world we made long ago. i won't ever be able to give you security, just a controlled chaos that would keep you safe and away from anyone trying to hurt you in any way. you're a brand new day for the dead i harbor and carry inside of me. i've tried burying everything as you did, but even the loss of you grows flowers i've learned to love and new earth to lay upon. i look at you and know my light doesn't sit in your eyes anymore. i know it won't be long until the ring on your finger weighs a little more, which means my vows, the ones i had been writing for you before you left, will amount to nothing but wasted promises to love you through death itself. i'm not jealous of him. i'm in a constant state of wondering, knowingly losing you and the moon at the same time. no one told me life would be like this, as if death sat upon my eyes and forced an image upon them of what being in love can do to those who end up alone by the time your breath becomes a weight you cannot get out of your lungs.

i could miss you for the next lifetime that finds us and it would still fall short of what i'm trying to keep alive for you. i could tell you i've been struggling, but even in the defeat, i'll continue getting back up on my feet if it means staying close to you. i could open up about the grief i've been keeping in, hoping healing begins where goodbye greeted us. maybe next time these scars will stay silent instead of speaking openly about the death they once represented. i know there were things we never said because time became something we lost and forgot how to use. you were the one who taught me how to love myself. i wish i had told you distance still feels like coming home where two arms are enough to hold it all together. everything you didn't say, became the words i write today.

be with the moon, sweet light.
better dreams await you tonight.
carefree and splendid, take these
wings and feel the wind, safely.
angels have a sense of love no
human could ever grant you.

there's still a part of me that will go down in flames to get to you. burning through the sun and finding a way to make everything else free from this pain. i am my own way, a sight not made for the eyes of angels and gods. i may be a lost boy, but you will never be far away.

i wanted to be honest about my life and where my head has been. it gets dark for me, more so during the holidays. it is a feeling of unworthiness for my achievements. a feeling of not being good enough for myself or anyone in my life. killing myself was something i tried over a decade ago. it won't ever be something i try again. but i do find it during my day without trying, without caring what tomorrow looks like. today feels black, burned, and already salvaged for the good that once sat beside me when all i had was a thousand acres to clear and build these dreams on.

one day i'll believe someone when they ask me to stay. one day i'll believe i'm good enough to keep this smile permanently on my face. one day the runner inside of me will die and being still in love becomes more than the poetry i write. when you grow up with the door left open and wide, you are perpetually haunted and hunted by the silhouettes left behind. their etchings become lessons, expressions and emotions you digest to keep from starving when pain becomes a hunger only loss can satisfy.

love is nothing if not everything. i'm a collapsing star, a thunderstorm awaiting lightning to strike me down to feel your touch once more. ease into it all, except when it comes to the one you call upon when existing becomes something beyond a passing blow. a poet's best friend is a memory that eats away at the soul, leaving words never found until the aching shows up ready for its feast. i'll stand in the rain if it means drowning for something more than the dryness of life without you.

and i thought how beautiful it was to have
something no one else had. not all things
will stay with you in your life. if you're
lucky, you may just find something
that chooses to.

A Poet's Degree in Suffering

may you rise like a prayer given at the birth of redemption. you've been a pillar for so long you forgot how it feels to fall, to land softly beside a reason to rest. when you were younger, all you knew how to do was fight for survival. to give yourself to the chaos. you believed in happy endings and heroes being the stars and a full moon. you stayed up long after everyone else was asleep, hoping to catch a few peaceful moments before life became something you couldn't control. but you kept finding ways to not only improve yourself, you restarted a heart that was emptied each time someone asked more from you. you were born a wonderling, a true image of victory and the second coming of Selene.

all it is about, is love, even when nothing else can hold you, console you, keep you from holding back, it is love. i've only been destroyed by it once, and even then, i'd give my scars back in return for more. heaven and hell are the two extremes we exist in. i'm somewhere in the middle trying to figure out the difference when at times they both feel the same.

starting over is nothing more than finding a better way to live when a newly held beginning dies right in front of you. you may think there is nothing left out there for you, then you stumble over a sunset and witness what can come from a death you kept mourning with a heaviness only meant for the heartless.

i still remember the stories you told me. all in, all the time, until oceans filled in what your hands failed to do. a golden glory washed an emboldened moment from the sun above. you told me about love as if you had never felt it before my hands pressed gently against your cheek, before kissing each scar that found me. i remember you spoke more about dreams than any dreamer i had ever met. the stars have always been another language for you. you use them to express yourself when being human is too much to put into words. the moon is your mother and you've learned all your secrets from her. you're a steady breath, a perfect gravity for all things living and dead. you'll forever be the girl who is ten minutes late just to see who stays for you when being late is still on time in a world that never sleeps.

A Poet's Degree in Suffering

there are days when i feel i have nothing left to give. days when i don't to share a single thing about me or tell anyone where i am with my heart and mind. i wake up already exhausted, depleted, and sore from my dreams and nightmares clashing. i'm tired of having your memory keep me hostage and unable to live a life free of regrets that aren't all mine. you need to let me go. you need to forget about me as a friend, as a human, as someone who can keep you in an embrace when my arms need to be holding onto things that make me better without feeling defeated. your life has no room for how i feel about you. i'm not sure it ever did. each time i think about you, i break a little more. i'm beyond the point of being anything other than who i need when it comes to my soulmate. my journey now is the open road and writing about those i come across in towns where no one knows me. being a stranger again is what i'll always be. a backpack and pages unwritten, coffee in the mornings, afternoons, and evenings.

i've been holding my breath since you left,
wishing things would change, but nothing
goes back in the same place once love
rearranges your face. i've been stuck
here for days, imagining a disaster,
picturing empty hands but holding a weapon
nonetheless. down dirt roads and open
fields full of ponds and recreational
dreaming, a virginity was lost and Jesus
drowned in the water beside us all.
this mind of mine is my tool and my coffin.
i'm only alive once i'm inside of it,
trapped and afraid to leave anything behind.
i'm the magician who hid his entire life
before you showed me the greatest trick of
all. i learned from you how to fly into the
sun and eat my way through until being full
meant being alive; steadily starving,
hauntingly existing by your side.

A Poet's Degree in Suffering

you were such a quiet thing. most of the time i forgot you were hurting because your smile was saving more than the day itself. i remember when we first met, your hands clenched around mine as if you knew what i had been through, as if you never wanted to lose me. you gave me protection through a connection i had never had before. you showed me life gives its toughest battles to those who were born with a heart unfit to be housed inside of a body. you became a daring darling, a woman of immense victory based on your own will to write a new story someone else was trying to finish for you. i'm not sure anyone knows you like i do. you removed the rope around my neck and led me down to safety. if loving you is the end of me, take me now. all i'll ever do when it comes to you, when it comes this endless love, is fall.

may your face never wear tears from the pain. i can only hope you walk in the rain, bearing your soul for the storm to feel how a human consists of love, even if it is broken and dangling from the stars inside of you. your worth is not what happens to you. it is predicated on how you make yourself feel on days when feeling nothing at all becomes a home your body doesn't fit in anymore. may your blessings become nameless and keep you from acquiring anymore scars than you already have.

i hope you know your place in this universe. i hope you never put yourself second to anything. firstly and lastly, it comes to you and the belief you have in everything beautiful finds you in cycles. it is the one thing that makes you who you are when someone asks about your story. you are the theory no man can ever attain. there are prisons and then there are structures where all the devils are kept. each one remains tortured by the thought of believing they know who you are, and for some, believing you could ever love them.

and then it all comes back to you.

maybe not as you planned it,

but new beginnings always bring a

certain kind of beauty with them.

i hope you never tire from the

feeling of belonging, of overcoming

what you thought would kill you.

i almost waited too long to become myself.
i left who i needed to be when i was young
behind me, just like the hands that did so
much wrong. i want to move on. i need to
move on away from everything reminding me
of what we've done. i never gave myself a
chance to grow up properly. i mishandled
anyone who got close to me, because i grew
up watching what never turned into love.
i wake up some days, begging for something
more to find me, begging for a direction i
need to start making my way to. i have
overcome so much and there are still ways
i can do more, while becoming a brighter
color than the sun. i broke my body and
promises for too many humans over the years.
it's time i actually heal from the carnage
and redirect my energy to clearing out a
new path for my words, my work, and myself.
i know i won't find you again, but whatever
i do find, it will be marvelous til the end.

finished my taxes for the year.

i got a five dollar refund as well as a life story from my CPA. there was a time, years ago, when i wasn't sure if we would ever have face to face conversations with someone ever again. i'm grateful for the small talk found in stores, on the streets, and inside of a tax office. near the end of her story, she began tearing up and apologized for doing so. i smiled and told her, thank you for giving me what i've been without for a while from strangers. i hope one day i can make it to Oregon where she told me about a speed boat her grandfather built in the thirties he used to race on the lake. a place where a museum showcases what life used to be for dreamers.

i love you, because you always find me, regardless of the silence i was born with. you never once shied away from me and who i was. if it were different, i wouldn't be who i am now. in a lot of ways, i owe my life to you. not in the gesture itself, but in the way the sun gives life to all light either caught or passing through. you are the one with hands that built the moon and gave mountains a reason to rise. i wasn't trying to scare you away, but even monsters become frightened of those who fight to try and love them anyway. i never had someone dig me up and remove the earth i had been choking on. your love is the best love, and the only thing worth writing about. it is the only thing i care to take my time with to make sure it is fucking perfect from all sides of the world.

your smile looks like it's been through a darkness not everyone can understand. there's still life left in it with enough light to make a dying star shine for another hundred wishes i'll send to you. each scar you've been given and earned, is one i will wear alongside the ones i already own. there is hope in the broken, in the misspoken who claim to be free while dying like the rest of us. before i ever held you, i could barely hold onto anything. i didn't believe in my strength until you said, i love you, too. we may never get an another day with each other, but we all take the risk once we exchange our stories about life and death to someone.

i once saw heaven in a daydream and you were standing before the gates with a god's smile and glance. you asked me what i was doing there. i laughed and asked you the same. a while back, you were once alive in a reality spaced out in-between a solidarity of primal truth and fiction. your body was an amenity for the starvation taking place within my borders of insanity and intrinsically placed love. we were destined to fall, but we shot the devil in the head and took its place amongst the thieves in this retreating world. now you and i stand face to face, guarding gates and dying for change. you are the amen after every saving grace.

it's been a long road for you. one without any light to see or speak to. beneath the breeze and old pine trees, you move as quickly as night in an attempt to take back what the day had stolen away from your pride. a wind strong moon you've always been, harboring a secret strength others have been drawn to. you belong to no one, making you an outlaw to everyone who doesn't understand you. you've guarded a heart worthy enough to be full at all costs. you've fended and fought off every devil aiming to take you out. courage looks different to each human, but to me, it's you. the only difference there is, lies within a reason for surviving versus a reason for defending and killing an intruder breaking into your soul for gold not belonging to them. you've always been the well i reside beside, my source of unbounded thirst.

i know one day, this love i have for you will make the earth in you shake. i found my place, twisted and tied off to your ribcage. there are scars of you on the scars of me. i've fought my entire fucking life to find you and i'll die to keep you safe. i hope the only thing others remember me for is how i tried to write you with a smile when i knew you were falling apart where you stood. not every woman will let you in to see the walls she's made. be there for her, incessantly, as resplendently imposing with your graceful approach to living. there are no lies within these lines i write for you only. may your hands always hold the flowers you deserve. may your smile always bring back those who have gone mad for a life they forgot how to live.

find the love that breaks you and keeps breaking you until you are all over the universe, screaming out for me. it is the only thing this life gives you that you can come back from, even when you feel your insides rejecting anything resembling another try.

you never know what you're capable of

until someone shows you the love and belief

you've been without your entire life.

it is never about approval. it is being

accepted by your own misconception

of who others told you you were before

you outgrew their lies.

i wanted you to love me more than anyone had tried before. i never asked you, because if i would have, i knew i would be asking for the rest of my life. once you begin down that road, it's a one lane highway where lovers go to die. if it needs to be said, chances are it's not in them from the beginning, and you both end up losing more than you're prepared to give. my curse is that i love everything and i think it loves me back all the same. my insanity is evident. i found the evidence in you.

i've watched love leave me like a summer's sigh before catching my second wind again. i've flown over buildings to get a better view of you as you continued on without me. i'm no closer to who my parents wanted me to be, but freedom becomes the chase and the chase becomes a deeper meaning once love spits you out one last time. i could say i miss you. i could say i need you. i could say my heart wanders in an empty body without yours next to it to keep it company. i could live another hundred years trying to get you to understand how much you've always been a part of me. when you are born, you have no idea what you're in for. you can only hope you don't get strangled by the same rope someone uses to help you out of the hell you'll find yourself later on in life. death and hard times are promises unbroken. you were my bind between bond and bone. you remain my deepest of breaths.

i don't want to past time just to die wasting the only gift that makes sense to open every day. it's not a pastime i'd prefer, when living with your eyes wide keeps your hunger young and at full stride. maybe in a past life, kings and queens became satisfied by holding golden thrones in open rooms wearing silk robes. i am not of the fabric meant to be worn by normal folks with a glass half-empty approach. i'm the one to run naked in the rain, wearing nudity as an escape from a painful life. i was the sapling caught underneath the underbrush, and you, you were the storm who moved and cleared branches once keeping light from touching me. this is why i love you. when humans speak of that word, they often refer to someone, but you are an event, a natural salvation.

A Poet's Degree in Suffering

i wonder if you still smile before you wake up. the half open glance you see the sun's first light through. there is love holding me together, even though i swore it off after your departure, after my drinking was called off, shot, beheaded, and buried. i've been told to let go of all of you, but my heart has a hard time deciding between your life or mine. if keeping you alive keeps me from finding someone else, it'll be a choice i'll make every single time. not everyone can be Hemingway, Neruda, Cohen, or Rilke. there are no more Kerouacs, Ginsbergs, or Cassadys. i am my own spirit, man, a fading dot on a map over-saturated with unbearable losses. whatever i remain to you, my poetry or self will never willingly kill his muse. there is no reward for such a thing. there is only victory for my angels to sing. my hand in yours, a delicate promise with burning wings. i am yours until you leave me. retreat does not accompany me. you're my infinite fixation, a collection of unsaid prayers before storming the gates.

i found love the day you found your way to me. before this world gave me purpose, it gave me your name. the devil tried to take me and dance away with my soul, but my hands and yours weren't made for letting go. life began making sense when breaking changed to bending and healing became holding onto you.

i may never know love as i know it to be with you. a place where nakedness and hope combine to mean a holy investment of who we are and what we wish to be. it won't be easy, but forever only asks those capable of sacrifice. where we end up together is a place i want to see when these beggary eyes answer the lonely i've seen in yours.

may you never go without what you need. may you always look to the moon and her children above when you feel doubt tap your shoulder to ask you if you feel like yourself. life is as cruel as we make it out to be, as we see the pain inflicted onto others. you were born with wild wings. i hope you never settle for anything less than magic and adventure, regardless of where you find yourself on any given day. you are the mountain, the wolf, and all of the light the moon needs. there will always be regret embedded within our bones. as soon as chaos birthed us, it knew we would never return, because we understood how being beautifully broken is love in its most authentic state.

the battles we go through may never give the answer we are looking for, but they will give us purpose. always remember to find your breath, to find your center. not all of us are meant or made for this world. not all of us will come to know a truth that will satisfy the ache we feel. we are created to find ourselves and a reason to go along with out desire for unearthly things. i need you to know how important you are, how much you matter, how you are not only a singular light, but you are my world. you are the sun and moon to my skies. you are every good thing that's happened to me. should you ever doubt any of this or fault yourself for not feeling human, come to me. i'll hold you and love you until your world is bright. i will give my life to loving all of the demons out of you.

i didn't want you to leave, to break me like a promise shared between stranger and friend. i didn't want to see you with him, but not all loves are meant to be kept in the light of the moon. some things you never come back from, like a kiss that makes the sunlight hurt less. i remember the first sunset when i visited you. the heat from the pavement. the way you ran to me as if you had once lost me before. i've never picked up the world before, until gathering you in arms that forgot how to hold onto anything except pain and loss from a life before you. i wanted forever. all i got was a memory for when i'm alone and being tormented becomes a life i didn't know one could survive. i never knew how to corral who i was until i saw you run free, running into me.

A Poet's Degree in Suffering

i know a brighter day will find you, a finer time when living isn't choking light out of you. i know you've met the devil before, back during your days of worry and exhaustion. you may feel departed and forgotten, but angels still find you through your darkest of apprehensions brought on by your inability to separate fact from fiction. there is feeding to be done. may your heart be spoiled and full by summer's end.

i always end up in someone else's life that doesn't need what i offer. i fall too fast when the other person has yet to reach the edge. i'm trying to understand fully not everyone will want what you have. they may want parts of what makes you the way you are and that's all. my downfall comes when i think they want something more or at least what i do. it's the greatest ache there is when you feel something for someone who doesn't feel it at all. my expectations always outweigh the reality. more times than not, i break my own fucking heart. i'll be changing that as i move into this new phase of my life. what's meant to be in your life won't ever ask you to stay. they will keep showing up without telling you. i just need someone who wakes up next to me, feeling what i feel for them. that's all. maybe i'm too simple of a man, but those are the most important parts of life to me.

A Poet's Degree in Suffering

love me like this, from where you are.
i am tired and alone, but not dead yet.
i am lonely and reflecting, but not moving
forward yet. miles are still left for me to
travel before my hands find earth to dig in,
to play in, to place these seeds i've been
keeping safe like sacred secrets. give me
a love like this, like the one i see in
your eyes for all of the times you could've
quit, but loved beyond your bones. my soul
has your heart safely placed next to each
seed i give back to the places that gave me
something to write about.

take me down to the song of your soul.
give me one last kiss, one last touch,
one last dance. my feet only know this
mumbled earth below me. i am in need
of your chaos to rattle these
caged bones of mine.

i still don't know how to hold you properly. my hands are still getting used to touching art, beauty, and a love like yours. i want you to be good. i want you to be okay with how much you have already done. do not belittle yourself or discredit everything that's brought you here. this is a place you never thought you would be able to make it to. there is always beauty in the struggle. there is always gold to find in the broken parts of life. the hurt you feel is not yours to carry alone. i know before you had to, but not anymore. i know how it feels to be alone with your grief, with a wounded animal living inside and all it does is scream. i am not here to change any part of you. i am here to tell you that you do not have to sit in an empty grave, waiting on everything you love to catch up and join you. live now while the sun is fresh and the moon still has shine to her name.

hold me close and tell me i am good enough.
hold me tight and remind me i am not what
my thoughts speak out loud. i am an
overly sensitive creature at times. i feel
too much or barely feel the bearing winds.
i do not seek out validation from you.
i come fully prepared and battle-tested.
i know myself well enough to ask for help
and embracement when i feel lonely tapping
on my shoulder. i am nothing more than
a human of needs.

the sun clings to your light. it learned
all of its power from you and your
glistening vibrations. you speak and the
sky shifts towards you. you are the only
woman i have ever met that created and
gave me a brand new day.

may the moon always know your shine, your life, your immense gift of being all soul. your light has been tested a few times too many, but here you stand, ready and willing to go toe to toe with anyone trying to cause you harm. you're all things glory. you were born for a greatness not many will ever know. you were made for these storms. you chase them all, even when the rains wash away the love. you are a wildness given to wolves to use for the moon and all of her stars. you are the home for every flower sentenced to live without adoration. you give breath its name and hold every heart of the broken in place.

i may never be more than enough for myself, and that is how the wind will blow for me. that is how the birds will rise for the raising sun in me. i have nail marks in the palms of my hands where life tried to crucify me for being authentic and raw to the bone with my feelings. i am not like you. i will not bend a knee to weaken my body, my stance, my forwardness. take me as i am or do not fucking step near me with a coward's tongue and face. i've died more times than you've attempted to live. my heart is still learning how not to eat itself. my soul is still learning how to control the lions within me. my atonement became the love we shared, after ruining my insides on cheap whiskey to burn out the demons i was forced to put there.

i wish i knew how to go slow. i wish i knew how to escape the paradox of needing love, but made to be a loner. i aim my sights on the moon most nights. it is the only time i know how to breathe before typing out these half-hearted goodbyes. she knows my intentions are pure, even though my insides are rotten to the core from the idea that love can save us in the end. i wish i knew how to make sense of what i feel for you. i wish i could speak with a braver face made of golden light and nectar squeezed from dying galaxies from afar. i am out here chasing lions and wolves from their homes, just so i can have something more to lose. love left me when you walked away and i've been walking in circles ever since. this time i will be amble, in life, in pursuit, in breath and with a poet's degree in suffering. you were an idea, a belief, an abounding bond of sound and touch. in my head you were a made up thing, but goddamn, could you love.

www.ingramcontent.com/pod-product-compliance
Lightning Source LLC
Chambersburg PA
CBHW011151290426
44109CB00025B/2569